Encouraging
Thoughts
for Women:
Hope

© 2013 by Barbour Publishing, Inc.

Written and compiled by Marjorie Vawter.

Some content previously appeared in *Everyday Hope*, published by Barbour Publishing, Inc. Used by permission.

Print ISBN 978-1-62416-138-4

eBook Editions:
Adobe Digital Edition (.epub) 978-1-62416-433-0
Kindle and MobiPocket Edition (.prc) 978-1-62416-432-3

Published by Barbour Publishing, Inc., PO Box 719, Uhrichsville, Ohio 44683, www.barbourbooks.com

Our mission is to publish and distribute inspirational products offering exceptional value and biblical encouragement to the masses.

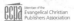

Member of the
Evangelical Christian
Publishers Association

Printed in the United States of America.

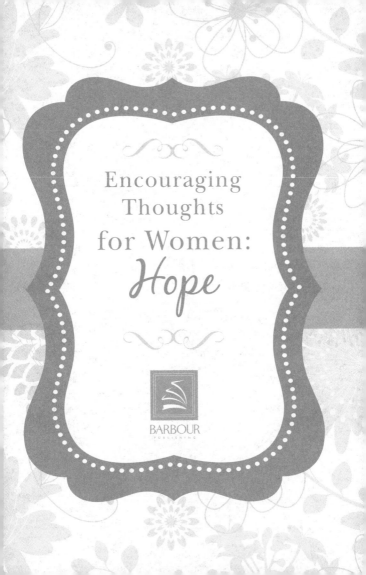

Encouraging
Thoughts
for Women:
Hope

BARBOUR
PUBLISHING

Contents

Introduction

*Faith is the confidence that what
we hope for will actually happen;
it gives us assurance about
things we cannot see.*
HEBREWS 11:1 NLT

We often use the word *hope* as a wish,
wanting a certain outcome but uncertain it
will happen that way. The actual definition of
hope is a "desire accompanied by expectation
of or belief in fulfillment." Not only is *hope*
a longing for something we fully expect to
happen—the anticipation of heaven for
the believer, for example—but it is also
an expectation that life has meaning and
purpose, which is found only in Jesus Christ.
Hope is a deep-down trust in our Abba Father
that has roots from before the foundation
of the world and extends into eternity. It is
trust, confidence, dependence, faith, refuge,
expectation, and strength all wrapped into one
word—*hope*. May your hope be strengthened
as you read these pages.

Abundant
Living

The thief enters only to steal, kill, and destroy.
I came so that they could have life—indeed,
so that they could live life to the fullest.
JOHN 10:10 CEB

Several times in Jesus' earthly ministry, He used examples from everyday life in first-century Israel to teach a spiritual truth. In John 10, He told the story of a shepherd coming to care for His flock. Jesus described a common practice of keeping the sheep within the household walls, so that the porter controlled who went in and out of the fold. Even if a stranger managed to get past the porter and into the pen with the sheep, they would ignore him. The sheep only have ears for their master's voice.

When the disciples didn't understand what Jesus wanted them to learn from the parable, He told it again in greater detail, in terms they could understand. The thief, Satan, only wants in the fold to steal, kill, and destroy. Jesus contrasted that with why He came. . . . So that every person could live a full, abundant life that doesn't end here on earth but continues on into eternity.

Jesus wasn't talking about material possessions but of His followers' spiritual life. He came to give us life—full, abundant, and free—forever. Like a well of water, it springs up within us and overflows onto those around us. Life with Jesus is more than we could ever imagine. And the abundance never, ever ends.

I pray that God, the source of hope,
will fill you completely with joy
and peace because you trust in him.
Then you will overflow with
confident hope through the
power of the Holy Spirit.
ROMANS 15:13 NLT

I, Paul, am an apostle on
special assignment for Christ,
our living hope.
1 TIMOTHY 1:1 MSG

Their faith and this knowledge
are based on the hope of
eternal life that God,
who doesn't lie,
promised before time began.
TITUS 1:2 CEB

Man can live about forty
days without food, about
three days without water,
about eight minutes without air,
but only for one
second without hope.

HAL LINDSEY

Strong hope is a much
greater stimulant of life than
any realized joy could be.

FRIEDRICH NIETZSCHE

Of all the forces that
make for a better world,
none is so indispensable,
none so powerful, as hope.
Without hope people are
only half alive. With hope they
dream and think and work.

CHARLES SAWYER

Dancing in the Puddles

And so, Lord,
where do I put my hope?
My only hope is in you.
PSALM 39:7 NLT

They say you can tell a lot about a
person's foundation of hope by the way she
handles a rainy day. Does she turn into a
gloomy Gussy, wailing, "Oh, woe is me. . ."
or does she make the best of a bad situation?
A hope-filled person will realize that abundant
life in Christ isn't about simply enduring
the storm but also about learning to dance
in the puddles. So grab your galoshes,
and let's boogie!

Source of Hope

✳

Father God, You are our
source of hope. Because
of Jesus, we can expect
to live full, satisfying lives,
not only here on earth
but also for eternity in heaven.
Fill us to overflowing with
Your joy and peace because
of the confident hope
we have through Your
indwelling Holy Spirit.
May this hope draw those
around us to faith and hope
in You. In Jesus' name, amen.

*To them God has chosen
to make known among
the Gentiles the glorious
riches of this mystery,
which is Christ in you,
the hope of glory.*

COLOSSIANS 1:27 NIV

✳

*Yes, this anguish was good
for me, for you have rescued
me from death and forgiven
all my sins. For the dead
cannot praise you; they cannot
raise their voices in praise.
Those who go down to the
grave can no longer hope
in your faithfulness.
Only the living can praise you
as I do today.*

ISAIAH 38:17–19 NLT

The life of the godly is full
of light and joy,
but the light of the wicked
will be snuffed out.
PROVERBS 13:9 NLT

May the God and Father of our
Lord Jesus Christ be blessed!
On account of his vast mercy,
he has given us new birth.
You have been born anew into
a living hope through the resurrection
of Jesus Christ from the dead.
1 PETER 1:3 CEB

"A thief is only there to steal and
kill and destroy. I [Jesus] came so
they can have real and eternal life,
more and better life than they
ever dreamed of."
JOHN 10:10 MSG

17

Shouts of Joy

He will yet fill your mouth
with laughter and your lips
with shouts of joy.
JOB 8:21 NIV

Do you remember the last time you laughed
till you cried? For many of us, it's been far too
long. Stress tends to steal our joy, leaving us
humorless and oh-so-serious. But lightness and
fun haven't disappeared forever. They may be
buried beneath the snow of a long, wintery life
season, but spring is coming, girls. Laughter
will bloom again, and our hearts will soar as
our lips shout with joy. Grasp that hope!

Laughter, the Best Medicine

✳

Gracious Father, we thank You for the gifts
of hope and laughter. Too often we allow the
struggles and sorrows of life to steal the hope
that lies within us. Jesus said He came to bring
us life—a life that abounds in hope. A life that
is more than we could ever dream or imagine
outside of Him. A life that overflows to those
who need Your hope and peace. Amen.

You are not here merely to
make a living. You are here in
order to enable the world to live
more amply, with greater vision,
with a finer spirit of hope and
achievement. You are here to
enrich the world, and you
impoverish yourself if
you forget the errand.

WOODROW T. WILSON

Where there's life,
there's hope.

TERENCE

Confidence

But let us who live in the light be clearheaded,
protected by the armor of faith and love,
and wearing as our helmet the
confidence of our salvation.

1 Thessalonians 5:8 nlt

When David took on Goliath's challenge
to fight to the death, King Saul attempted
to dress the young shepherd in his adult-
sized armor. Notice Saul didn't attempt to
stop David, but he refused to send him out
without more protection than David's everyday
clothing. After he tried the armor, David took
it off, saying he hadn't tested it (1 Samuel 17).
Saul's armor would only hamper David rather
than help. He was comfortable and confident
in his own clothes.

On the cross Jesus paid the only price God would accept to cover our sins—His perfect lifeblood. The gift of salvation is free for all who will take it. At the same time God issues a full suit of armor to each of His children. He knows how fierce the battle can be against the enemy of our souls. And because the battle is fiercest in our minds, the helmet is key to protecting them.

Paul compared the helmet to ones worn by the Roman soldiers (Ephesians 6). This helmet was the warrior's most valuable, ornate, and expensive piece of equipment, complete with flaps that covered the cheeks, so it protected the entire head. When we accept Christ's payment on the cross for our sins, God gives us a similar helmet. All we have to do is put it on.

For I hope in You, O LORD;
You will answer, O Lord my God.
PSALM 38:15 NASB

Why am I discouraged?
Why is my heart so sad?
I will put my hope in God!
I will praise him again—
my Savior and my God!
PSALM 42:11 NLT

For You are my hope; O Lord GOD, You
are my confidence from my youth.
PSALM 71:5 NASB

How blessed is he whose help
is the God of Jacob, whose hope
is in the LORD his God.
PSALM 146:5 NASB

Optimism is the faith that leads to achievement. Nothing can be done without hope and confidence.

HELEN KELLER

You are as young as your faith, as old as your doubt; as young as your self-confidence, as old as your fear; as young as your hope, as old as your despair.

SAMUEL ULLMAN

History informs us of past mistakes from which we can learn without repeating them. It also inspires us and gives confidence and hope bred of victories already won.

WILLIAM HASTIE

Getting to Know You

For the law never made anything perfect.
But now we have confidence in a better hope,
through which we draw near to God.

HEBREWS 7:19 NLT

Following Old Testament law used to be
considered the way to achieve righteousness,
but obeying rules just doesn't work for fallible
humans. We mess up. We fail miserably. Then
Jesus came and provided a better way to draw
near to God. He bridged the gap by offering
us a personal relationship rather than rules.
Together we laugh, cry, love, grieve, rejoice.
We get to know our Papa God through
our personal relationship with Him.

Praise Him

Father, we are so easily
discouraged by events and
circumstances we cannot
control. They touch on
emotions and trigger
symptoms of depression
and anxiety within us.
It seems as though no one
desires to seek You and Your
solutions to the problems we
face. But when we do look to
You and seek to praise You in
spite of our circumstances,
Your hope infuses our souls
and minds. And we cannot
help but praise You. Amen.

"Is not your fear of God your confidence, and the integrity of your ways your hope?"

JOB 4:6 NASB

We can rejoice, too, when we run into problems and trials, for we know that they help us develop endurance. And endurance develops strength of character, and character strengthens our confident hope of salvation. And this hope will not lead to disappointment. For we know how dearly God loves us, because he has given us the Holy Spirit to fill our hearts with his love.

ROMANS 5:3–5 NLT

*For the law never made anything
perfect. But now we have confidence
in a better hope, through which
we draw near to God.*
HEBREWS 7:19 NLT

*I pray that your hearts will be flooded
with light so that you can understand
the confident hope he has given to those
he called—his holy people who are his
rich and glorious inheritance.*
EPHESIANS 1:18 NLT

Smiling in the Darkness

· ·

The hopes of the godless evaporate.
JOB 8:13 NLT

Hope isn't just an emotion; it's a perspective, a discipline, a way of life. It's a journey of choice. We must learn to override those messages of discouragement, despair, and fear that assault us in times of trouble and press toward the light. Hope is smiling in the darkness. It's confidence that faith in God's sovereignty amounts to something. . .something life-changing, life-saving, and eternal.

Abba Father

Lord, because of Christ's work on the cross we are restored to fellowship with You. Our bodies are the temple where Your Holy Spirit lives. And the hope and confidence He brings with Him gives us the courage to persevere in the path You have laid out before us. You are our Abba Father, and as a child confident of her father's love is not shy to climb into his lap and make her request of his beneficence, neither should we be. Amen.

Morale is the state of mind.
It is steadfastness and courage and hope.
It is confidence and zeal and loyalty.
It is élan, esprit de corps, and determination.

GENERAL GEORGE CATLETT MARSHALL

He who has faith has. . .an inward reservoir
of courage, hope, confidence, calmness,
and assuring trust that all will come out well—
even though to the world it may appear
to come out most badly.

B. C. FORBES

Jesus, my Strength, my Hope,
On Thee I cast my care,
With humble confidence look up,
And know Thou hear'st my prayer.

CHARLES WESLEY

Courage

*Always be prepared to give an answer
to everyone who asks you to give the
reason for the hope that you have.
But do this with gentleness and respect.*
1 PETER 3:15 NIV

"What makes you people different from everyone else on this unit?" a nurse asked the young husband as she tended to the critical needs of his wife.

For the past several weeks, his wife had fought off infection, disease, and the partial shutdown of several of her organs while waiting for a liver transplant. Several times the doctors had given up, thinking she would die before the night was over. But the call for prayer went out over social media, and people all over the world prayed for this young couple.

Because she'd been a patient in the medical intensive care unit for over two months, the staff had had ample time to observe her and the family as they passed through crisis after crisis without complaint, without railing against those who were trying to help with little success, without blaming God.

Having had lots of time for thinking, praying, and reading God's Word, the young man was prepared for the question when it came. His wife belonged to God wholly and completely. It was their deep-down desire that God would get the glory no matter what happened. And because of their faith in Jesus Christ and their hope of eternal life after this life, they were able to face this deep trial of their faith with peace and a strength that came from the Lord.

Having hope will give you courage.
You will be protected
and will rest in safety.
JOB 11:18 NLT

So be strong and courageous,
all you who put your hope in the LORD!
PSALM 31:24 NLT

The high and lofty one who lives in
eternity, the Holy One, says this:
"I live in the high and holy place with
those whose spirits are contrite and
humble. I restore the crushed spirit of
the humble and revive the courage of
those with repentant hearts."
ISAIAH 57:15 NLT

Wait for the LORD; be strong
and let your heart take courage;
yes, wait for the LORD.
PSALM 27:14 NASB

There is hope in dreams,
imagination, and in the courage
of those who wish to make
those dreams a reality.

JONAS SALK

The stories of past courage can
define that ingredient—they can
teach, they can offer hope, they
can provide inspiration. But they
cannot supply courage itself.
For this each man must look
into his own soul.

JOHN F. KENNEDY

If you lose hope, somehow you lose
the vitality that keeps life moving,
you lose that courage to be,
that quality that helps you go
on in spite of it all.

MARTIN LUTHER KING JR.

Bigger than Fear

Having hope will give you courage.
You will be protected and will rest in safety.
JOB 11:18 NLT

Tossing, turning, sleepless nights:
What woman doesn't know these intimately?
Our thoughts race with the "what ifs" and
fear steals our peace. How precious is God's
promise that He will rescue us from nagging,
faceless fear and give us courage to just say
no to anxious thoughts that threaten to
terrorize us at our most vulnerable moments.
He is our hope and protector.
He is bigger than fear. Anxiety flees in
His presence. Rest with Him tonight.

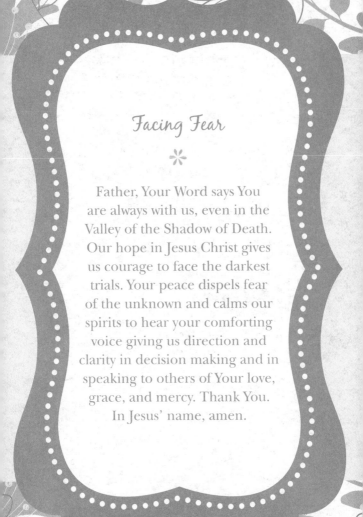

Facing Fear

✳

Father, Your Word says You
are always with us, even in the
Valley of the Shadow of Death.
Our hope in Jesus Christ gives
us courage to face the darkest
trials. Your peace dispels fear
of the unknown and calms our
spirits to hear your comforting
voice giving us direction and
clarity in decision making and in
speaking to others of Your love,
grace, and mercy. Thank You.
In Jesus' name, amen.

*I eagerly expect and hope that
I will in no way be ashamed, but will
have sufficient courage so that now as
always Christ will be exalted in my body,
whether by life or by death.*
PHILIPPIANS 1:20 NIV

*With that kind of hope to excite us,
nothing holds us back.*
2 CORINTHIANS 3:12 MSG

*But Jesus turning and seeing her said,
"Daughter, take courage; your faith
has made you well." At once the
woman was made well.*
MATTHEW 9:22 NASB

*Then you planted a flag to rally
your people, an unfurled flag
to look to for courage.*
PSALM 60:4 MSG

Tell fearful souls, "Courage! Take heart!
GOD is here, right here, on his way to put
things right and redress all wrongs.
He's on his way! He'll save you!"
ISAIAH 35:4 MSG

"Be strong. Take courage. Don't be
intimidated. Don't give them a second
thought because GOD, your God, is
striding ahead of you. He's right there
with you. He won't let you down;
he won't leave you."
DEUTERONOMY 31:6 MSG

"Will your courage endure or your hands
be strong in the day I deal with you?
I the LORD have spoken,
and I will do it."
EZEKIEL 22:14 NIV

No Wimps Here

For God has not given us a spirit of fear and timidity, but of power, love, and self-discipline.
2 TIMOTHY 1:7 NLT

Do you suffer paralysis by analysis?
Are you so afraid of trying something new
that you put it off until you can think it
through. . .and end up doing nothing at all?
Too much introspection creates inertia, and
we abhor the ineffective wimps we become.
Sisters, God never intended for us to be wimps.
His power and love are available to replace
our fear and infuse us with courage.
Shake off that paralysis and get moving!

Facing Fear

Lord, it's so easy to allow fear
to keep us from moving forward
in life. Fear of an illness, fear
of how others perceive us, fear
of something new, fear of the
unknown, fear of inadequacy. Help
us remember that courage isn't the
absence of fear; it's pressing on in
spite of it. It helps to know You are
right beside us, reminding us that
Your perfect love casts out fear.
Keep our eyes on Jesus today.

Courage is like love; it must have
hope to nourish it.

NAPOLEON BONAPARTE

Hope has two beautiful daughters;
their names are anger and courage.
Anger that things are the way they are.
Courage to make them the way they ought to be.

SAINT AUGUSTINE

Whatever enlarges hope will also exalt courage.

SAMUEL JOHNSON

Woe is me if I do not preach the Gospel;
if I did not aim at that and possess faith and
hope in Christ, it would be bad for me indeed,
but no, I have some courage.

VINCENT VAN GOGH

Future

The lines of purpose in your lives never grow slack,
tightly tied as they are to your future
in heaven, kept taut by hope.
COLOSSIANS 1:5 MSG

Have you ever wondered what God's purpose is for you, whether here on earth or in our future home in heaven? The apostle Paul, formerly known as Saul, knew exactly what God's purpose was for stopping him on the road to Damascus. Those three days after his encounter with Jesus must have been one intense conversation with his new Master. After all, Saul's life radically changed from "breathing threats and murder against the disciples of the Lord" to becoming "a chosen instrument" to bear Christ's name "before the Gentiles and kings and the sons of Israel" (Acts 9:1, 15 NASB). Even his name changed.

God has a plan, a purpose, for each one of us. It may not be as clear as it was for Paul, but we don't need to worry. The Lord will make it plain in His time. In the meantime, we can know that having the hope of salvation and eternal life in heaven is keeping those lines of purpose taut. He will never let us go; He will never let His purposes for us fade. As He told Israel in exile in Babylon, He also tells us today, "I know what I'm doing. I have it all planned out—plans to take care of you, not abandon you, plans to give you the future you hope for" (Jeremiah 29:11 MSG).

*And we believers also groan, even
though we have the Holy Spirit within
us as a foretaste of future glory, for we
long for our bodies to be released from
sin and suffering. We, too, wait with
eager hope for the day when God will
give us our full rights as his adopted
children, including the new bodies
he has promised us. We were given
this hope when we were saved.*

ROMANS 8:23–24 NLT

*Because of his grace he declared us
righteous and gave us confidence
that we will inherit eternal life.*

TITUS 3:7 NLT

I don't know about tomorrow;
It may bring me poverty.
But the one who feeds the sparrow,
Is the one who stands by me.
And the path that is my portion
May be through the flame or flood;
But His presence goes before me
And I'm covered with His blood.
Many things about tomorrow
I don't seem to understand
But I know who holds tomorrow
And I know who holds my hand.

IRA FOREST STAMPHILL

Beyond the Horizon

Always continue to fear the LORD.
You will be rewarded for this;
your hope will not be disappointed.
PROVERBS 23:17–18 NLT

Have you ever traversed a long, winding
road, unable to see your final destination?
Perhaps you were surprised by twists
and turns along the way or jarred by
unexpected potholes. But you were confident
that if you stayed on that road, you would
eventually reach your destination. Likewise,
God has mapped out our futures. The end of
the road may disappear beyond the horizon,
but we are assured that our destination
will not be disappointing.

Tomorrow

Gracious Lord, we may not know about tomorrow, but we do know the One who does. Sometimes You allow us glimpses, but You desire that we learn to leave the future in Your hands. You know the pitfalls as well as the delights. Your presence goes before us, behind us, and beside us. Surround us with Your peace that passes all understanding as we travel the path You have ordained for us. Amen.

And if our hope in Christ is only for this life, we are more to be pitied than anyone in the world.

1 Corinthians 15:19 NLT

For there is one body and one Spirit, just as you have been called to one glorious hope for the future.

Ephesians 4:4 NLT

We want you to know what will happen to the believers who have died so you will not grieve like people who have no hope.

1 Thessalonians 4:13 NLT

We wait for the blessed hope—the appearing of the glory of our great God and Savior, Jesus Christ.

Titus 2:13 NIV

*If we already have something, we
don't need to hope for it. But if we look
forward to something we don't yet have,
we must wait patiently and confidently.*
ROMANS 8:24–25 NLT

*Such things were written in the
Scriptures long ago to teach us.
And the Scriptures give us hope and
encouragement as we wait patiently for
God's promises to be fulfilled.*
ROMANS 15:4 NLT

*Keep yourselves in the love of God,
waiting anxiously for the mercy of our
Lord Jesus Christ to eternal life.*
JUDE 1:21 NASB

Keep Breathing, Sister!

* *

As long as we are alive, we still have hope,
just as a live dog is better off than a dead lion.
ECCLESIASTES 9:4 CEV

Isn't this a tremendous scripture?
At first glance, the ending elicits a chuckle.
But consider the truth it contains:
Regardless of how powerful, regal,
or intimidating a lion is, when he's dead,
he's dead. But the living—you and I—still
have hope. Limitless possibilities! Hope for
today and for the future. Although we may
be as lowly dogs, fresh, juicy bones abound.
As long as we're breathing, it's not too late!

End Times

Father, how we long for the soon return of Your Son, Jesus Christ! He said that as it was in the days of Noah so it will be when He returns. Each day the world seems to grow worse; sin is more open and rampant, even acceptable. Our loved ones are taken from us. Fools and mockers are our leaders. But through it all we have the bright hope of heaven before us. Even so, come quickly, Lord Jesus. Amen.

Be still, my soul! thy God doth undertake
To guide the future as he has the past.
Thy hope, thy confidence let nothing shake;
All now mysterious shall be bright at last.
Be still, my soul! the waves and
winds still know His voice who
ruled them while He dwelt below.

KATHARINA VON SCHLEGEL

God's Faithful Love

Yet I still dare to hope when I remember this:
The faithful love of the LORD never ends!
His mercies never cease. Great is his faithfulness;
his mercies begin afresh each morning.
LAMENTATIONS 3:21–23 NLT

Jeremiah wrote the book of Lamentations after
Nebuchadnezzar and his Babylonian army
ransacked Jerusalem the final time. Only a
remnant was left to live among the ruins of the
temple and the city. Everyone else was either
dead or on their way into exile in Babylon.

When God called Jeremiah to be His prophet and to preach warning after warning to Jeremiah's spiritually deaf countrymen, He told him that no one would listen to him. And no one did. Persecuted for his message, he was put in an old cistern in an attempt to silence him. His scribe, Baruch, faithfully wrote down the messages Jeremiah preached—only to have the king's men confiscate it and burn it at the king's orders. Baruch rewrote. And still no one listened.

The first twenty verses in Lamentations 3 are super depressing to read. But then, in verses 22 and 23, Jeremiah remembered a principle that caused his hope to burst forth anew: "The faithful love of the LORD never ends! His mercies never cease. Great is his faithfulness; his mercies begin afresh each morning" (NLT).

God's mercies and faithfulness are still available to His people today, many centuries later. They are still fresh every morning. In the direst of circumstances we have hope that one day it will be better. Great is His faithfulness.

*The Lord's delight is in those
who fear him, those who put their
hope in his unfailing love.*
PSALM 147:11 NLT

*This anguish was good for me, for
you have rescued me from death and
forgiven all my sins. For the dead
cannot praise you; they cannot raise
their voices in praise. Those who go
down to the grave can no longer hope
in your faithfulness. Only the living
can praise you as I do today.*
ISAIAH 38:17–19 NLT

*Love never gives up, never loses
faith, is always hopeful, and endures
through every circumstance.*
1 CORINTHIANS 13:7 NLT

Lord, make me an instrument of
your peace; where there is hatred,
let me sow love; where there is
injury, pardon; where there is
doubt, faith; where there is despair,
hope; where there is darkness,
light; and where there
is sadness, joy.

SAINT FRANCIS OF ASSISI

To love is to risk not being loved
in return. To hope is to risk pain.
To try is to risk failure, but risk
must be taken because the greatest
hazard in life is to risk nothing.

LEO BUSCAGLIA

Love, we say, is life; but love without
hope and faith is agonizing death.

ELBERT HUBBARD

Everyday Blessings
• • • • • • • • • • • • • • • • • • • •

But the eyes of the LORD are on those who fear him,
on those whose hope is in his unfailing love.

PSALM 33:18 NIV

The Lord of all creation is watching our
every moment and wants to fill us with His
joy. He often interrupts our lives with His
blessings: butterflies dancing in sunbeams,
dew-touched spiderwebs, cotton candy clouds,
and glorious crimson sunsets. The beauty of
His creation reassures us of His unfailing
love and fills us with hope. But it is up
to us to take the time to notice.

Love Never Fails

Loving Father, we praise You for
the ultimate measure of Your
love for us: You sent Your Son to
die for our sins. How do we repay
such a gift? We cannot. Yet in love
and gratitude for Your generosity
we can do nothing less than give
You our best. You are the perfect
example of unconditional love.
May our lives reflect that to a
lost and dying world. Amen.

Know therefore that the LORD
your God is God;
he is the faithful God, keeping his
covenant of love to a thousand
generations of those who love him
and keep his commands.
DEUTERONOMY 7:9 NIV

Your love, GOD, is my song, and I'll
sing it! I'm forever telling everyone
how faithful you are.
PSALM 89:1 MSG

Give thanks to the LORD, for he is
good! His faithful love endures forever.
1 CHRONICLES 16:34 NLT

Love the LORD, all you godly ones!
For the LORD protects those who
are loyal to him, but he harshly
punishes the arrogant.
PSALM 31:23 NLT

[Nehemiah] said: "LORD God of heaven, great and awesome God, you are the one who keeps covenant and is truly faithful to those who love you and keep your commandments."
NEHEMIAH 1:5 CEB

His love has taken over our lives; GOD's faithful ways are eternal. Hallelujah!
PSALM 117:2 MSG

Yes, goodness and faithful love will pursue me all the days of my life, and I will live in the LORD's house as long as I live.
PSALM 23:6 CEB

I Do
• • • • •

*Let us hold unswervingly to the hope we profess,
for he who promised is faithful.*
HEBREWS 10:23 NIV

An important part of any marriage is the
vow of faithfulness. We pledge that we will
remain faithful to our beloved until death do
us part. Faithfulness is crucial to a trusting
relationship. We must be able to depend on
our spouse to always be in our corner,
love us even when we're unlovable,
and never leave or forsake us.
God is faithful. We can unswervingly
depend on Him to never break His promises.

Faithful God

Father God, You are greatly to be praised for Your faithfulness to all generations. You are faithful in life, faithful in death, faithful in provision, faithful in strength, faithful in mercy, faithful in love. Every minute of every day Your faithfulness shines through. Open our eyes to see Your faithfulness in all You do. Every day Your mercies are new. Your grace is sufficient for each situation. We lift our arms in praise to You.

Our righteousness is in Him, and our hope
depends, not upon the exercise of grace in
us, but upon the fullness of grace and love in
Him, and upon His obedience unto death.

JOHN NEWTON

They say a person needs just three things to
be truly happy in this world: someone to love,
something to do, and something to hope for.

TOM BODETT

Love's redeeming work is done, Alleluia!
Fought the fight, the battle won, Alleluia!
Death in vain forbids Him rise, Alleluia!
Christ hath opened paradise, Alleluia!

CHARLES WESLEY

God's Word

You are my refuge and my shield;
I have put my hope in your word.
PSALM 119:114 NIV

The shield used by the Roman soldiers was no small, light piece of protection. Many were the size of doors, big enough to stand behind and be completely sheltered from a barrage of fiery arrows or long spears. Made of wood, they were then covered with leather. Before battle, the soldiers would soak the entire shield with water, making them fire resistant. . .and heavier. These soldiers weren't wimps!

Because of the size of the shields, the Romans presented a formidable line when coming against a walled city. An entire unit would band together to form a tank-like barrier to the archers and other soldiers on the walls above them. The soldiers on the outside of the formation would place their shields vertically, making a solid wall around the unit. The soldiers in the center placed their shields above them horizontally, completely sealing the men within a fire-resistant box. This allowed them to get close to the walls to assault the gates or any weak areas at the foundations without a great sacrifice of lives.

This is the type of refuge we find in God's Word. When we put our hope in the promises God has laid out in His love letter to us, His Word surrounds us and protects us from the onslaught of fiery darts the enemy throws our way. What an awesome picture of God's provision for our safety in any circumstance.

Remember your promise to me; it is my only hope.
PSALM 119:49 NLT

May those who fear you rejoice when they see me,
for I have put my hope in your word.
PSALM 119:74 NIV

God can't break his word. And because his word
cannot change, the promise is likewise unchangeable.
We who have run for our very lives to God
have every reason to grab the promised
hope with both hands and never let go.
HEBREWS 6:18 MSG

I am worn out waiting for your rescue,
but I have put my hope in your word.
PSALM 119:81 NLT

Waiting on God

Father, many times in the midst of a trial or battle, we find ourselves waiting on You. Waiting is hard, especially when we're surrounded by trouble and we need rescuing now. But the waiting is easier when You recall to our minds the promises of Your Word. Because You cannot lie, we can know You will come to our rescue, though it most likely will not be what we expect. Amen.

I am counting on the LORD; yes,
I am counting on him.
I have put my hope in his word.
PSALM 130:5 NLT

So let us seize and hold fast and retain
without wavering the hope we cherish
and confess and our acknowledgement
of it, for He Who promised is reliable
(sure) and faithful to His word.
HEBREWS 10:23 AMP

You have this faith and love because
of the hope reserved for you in heaven.
You previously heard about
this hope through the true message,
the good news.
COLOSSIANS 1:5 CEB

The Bible's words are our hope.

BILLY GRAHAM

Hope is the word which God has
written on the brow of every man.

VICTOR HUGO

Our Lord has written the promise
of resurrection, not in books alone,
but in every leaf in springtime.

MARTIN LUTHER

The church's one foundation
is Jesus Christ her Lord;
she is his new creation
by water and the Word.
From heaven he came and sought
her to be his holy bride;
with his own blood he bought
her, and for her life he died.

SAMUEL J. STONE

Questions and Answers

. . . .

*And the Scriptures were written to teach
and encourage us by giving us hope.*
ROMANS 15:4 CEV

What do you do when facing a perplexing
problem? Ask a family member? Consult
a friend? Turn to the Internet?
God's Word is brimming with answers to life's
difficulties, yet it's often the last place we
turn. God speaks to us today through the lives
of trusting Abraham, brokenhearted Ruth,
runaway Jonah, courageous Esther, female
leader Deborah in a male-dominated society,
beaten-down Job, double-crossing Peter, and
Paul, who proved people can change.

God Is Our Help

O God, so often the last place we
turn to for help in times of trouble
is where we should have gone in the
first place. Give us such a thirst
for Your Word that it saturates
every part of our being, giving us
relief sooner rather than later.
Your Word is our meat and bread
and contains the solutions to
every problem. Thank You for
this provision. We love You.

I was up before sunrise,
crying for help,
hoping for a word from you.
Psalm 119:147 MSG

But if anyone obeys his word,
love for God is truly made
complete in them.
This is how we know we are in him.
1 John 2:5 NIV

He that is of God heareth God's words.
John 8:47 KJV

For the word of the Lord holds true,
and we can trust everything he does.
Psalm 33:4 NLT

I wait for God, my soul doth wait;
My hope is in His Word.
More than they that
for morning watch,
My soul waits for the Lord.

Scottish Psalter, 1650

The Word of God well understood
and religiously obeyed is the
shortest route to spiritual
perfection. And we must not select
a few favorite passages to the
exclusion of others. Nothing less
than a whole Bible can
make a whole Christian.

A. W. Tozer

If You Build It, He Will Come

....

Do not snatch your word of truth from me,
for your regulations are my only hope.
Psalm 119:43 nlt

Bibles wear and tear. Papers get discarded.
Hard drives crash. But memorizing scripture
assures us that God's Word will never be lost.
His truth will always be at our disposal,
any moment of the day or night when we
need a word of encouragement, of guidance,
of hope. Like a phone call from heaven,
our Father communicates to us via
scripture implanted in our hearts.
But it is up to us to build the signal tower.

Sin and God's Word

Father, many of us have a quote written in the fronts of our Bibles saying, "This Book will keep you from sin, or sin will keep you from this Book." What a great reminder to keep us in Your Word. Sharpen our minds so we can commit scripture to memory—another guard against sin when we recall it at a time of temptation. Teach us how to wield the Sword effectively. In Jesus' name, amen.

It does not require great learning to be
a Christian and be convinced of the truth
of the Bible. It requires only an honest
heart and a willingness to obey God.

ALBERT BARNES

All who call on God in true faith, earnestly
from the heart, will certainly be heard, and
will receive what they have asked and desired.

MARTIN LUTHER

The Bible is one of the greatest blessings
bestowed by God on the children of men.
It has God for its author, salvation for its end,
and truth without any mixture for its matter.
It is all pure.

JOHN LOCKE

Joyful Living

Be joyful in hope, patient in affliction,
faithful in prayer.
ROMANS 12:12 NIV

Joyful in hope. Paul's letter to the Romans is a
essay on salvation in Christ Jesus alone, written
by a man who was skillfully trained in logic and
the Law. The first five chapters describe how
we are all condemned because of sin, how God
provided the needed sacrifice to pay our debt
to sin, and how that sacrifice satisfied the Law's
demands. The next three chapters show how
believers are molded and reshaped into the
image of Christ. After reading and studying
these chapters, it's difficult to suppress the joy
resulting from the incredible hope we can find
in Christ.

Patient in affliction. Paul's life is an example of patience in affliction. In his second letter to the Corinthians Paul lists the trials and difficulties he experienced since coming to know Christ as his Savior. "Labors. . .imprisonments. . .beaten. . .in danger of death. Five times. . .thirty-nine lashes. . .beaten with rods. . .I was stoned. . . shipwrecked," and many other dangers and trials (11:23–28 NASB). Are we willing to bear affliction for the cause of Christ?

Faithful in prayer. Paul's prayers are well documented in his letters to the churches. He pleaded with his readers to "pray at all times in the Spirit" (Ephesians 6:18), "pray without ceasing" (1 Thessalonians 5:17), and "to pray. . .without wrath and dissension" (1 Timothy 2:8). James tells us that "the effective prayer of a righteous man can accomplish much" (5:16). When we commit to pray for someone or for a situation, follow through. Prayer for one another strengthens not only the pray-er but also the entire body of believers.

I have set the LORD always before me:
because he is at my right hand, I shall not be moved.
Therefore my heart is glad, and my glory rejoiceth:
my flesh also shall rest in hope.
PSALM 16:8–9 KJV

May the God of green hope fill you up with joy,
fill you up with peace, so that your believing lives,
filled with the life-giving energy of the Holy Spirit,
will brim over with hope!
ROMANS 15:13 MSG

The hope of the righteous is gladness,
but the expectation of the wicked perishes.
PROVERBS 10:28 NASB

Joy

*

Father, there's nothing like
the deep-down joy imbedded
deep within our souls. It is the
undercurrent to life, running still
and deep, never failing. Sometimes
we bury it under the cares of
life; other times it bubbles out in
laughter and worship. It's more
than being happy, though it is a
close cousin to happiness. "Hope
springs eternal" is true when it
comes to the believer. What a
glorious hope we have in Christ!
Amen.

We put our hope in the L<small>ORD</small>.
He is our help and our shield.
In him our hearts rejoice, for we
trust in his holy name. Let your
unfailing love surround us, L<small>ORD</small>,
for our hope is in you alone.
P<small>SALM</small> 33:20–22 <small>NLT</small>

For who is our hope or joy
or crown of exultation?
Is it not even you,
in the presence of our
Lord Jesus at His coming?
1 T<small>HESSALONIANS</small> 2:19 <small>NASB</small>

No wonder my heart is glad,
and my tongue shouts his praises!
My body rests in hope.
A<small>CTS</small> 2:26 <small>NLT</small>

Come, Thou long expected Jesus
Born to set Thy people free;
From our fears and sins release us,
Let us find our rest in Thee.
Israel's Strength and Consolation,
Hope of all the earth Thou art;
Dear Desire of every nation,
Joy of every longing heart.

CHARLES WESLEY

A propensity to hope
and joy is real riches;
one to fear and sorrow
real poverty.

DAVID HUME

Rejoice in glorious hope!
Jesus the Judge shall come,
And take His servants up
to their eternal home.

CHARLES WESLEY

Pick Me Up, Daddy

We boast in the hope of the glory of God.
ROMANS 5:2 NIV

To rejoice means to live joyfully…joy-fully…
full of joy. Joy is a decision we make. A choice
not to keep wallowing in the mud of our
lives. And there will be mud—at one time or
another. When spiritual rain mixes with the
dirt of fallen people, mud is the inevitable
result. The Creator of sparkling sunbeams,
soaring eagles, and spectacular fuchsia
sunsets wants to lift us out of the mud.
Why don't we raise our arms to Him today?

Hope in Christ

Father God, we look forward
to the hope of Christ's coming
again. What a comfort and joy it
is to know we will be reunited with
our loved ones in Christ someday.
What a reunion we have to look
forward to. Because of Christ's
death and resurrection, the sting
of Death is gone, replaced by
the glorious hope of eternal life
with You. We will never cease
to praise You. Amen.

The Lord taketh pleasure
in them that fear him,
in those that hope in his mercy.
Psalm 147:11 kjv

This is the day which
the Lord has made;
Let us rejoice and be glad in it.
Psalm 118:24 nasb

Weeping may last for the night,
but a shout of joy comes
in the morning.
Psalm 30:5 nasb

The trouble with many men is that
they have got just enough religion
to make them miserable. If there is
not joy in religion, you have got
a leak in your religion.

BILLY SUNDAY

Your joy comes from
how you think, the choices
that we make in life.

JOYCE MEYER

We have within ourselves
Enough to fill the present
day with joy,
And overspread the future
years with hope.

WILLIAM WORDSWORTH

Soul Sister

• • • • • • • • • • • • •

I always see the Lord near me,
and I will not be afraid with him at my right side.
Because of this, my heart will be glad,
my words will be joyful, and I will live in hope.
ACTS 2:25–26 CEV

Laughter is the soul sister of joy; they often
travel together. Humor is the primary catalyst
for releasing joy into our souls and making our
hearts glad. It's healthy for us, too! Laughter
is cleansing and healing, a powerful salve for
the wounds of life. . .a natural medicine and
tremendous stress reliever. Laughing is to joy
what a 50% OFF sign is to shopping.
It motivates us to seek more, more, more!

A Living Hope

"O God, our help in ages past,
our hope for years to come." How
we praise You for the hope that
sustains life in us. Even when
earthly hopes disappoint and
fail us, You are always with us,
teaching us that true hope is found
only in Jesus Christ, the hope of
glory. This hope is alive, vibrant,
and eternal. All praise and glory
belong to You. Amen.

Hope is a state of mind, not of the world.
Hope, in this deep and powerful sense,
is not the same as joy that things are
going well, or willingness to invest in
enterprises that are obviously heading
for success, but rather an ability to work
for something because it is good.

VACLAV HAVEL

My spirits were elevated by the
enchanting appearance of nature;
the past was blotted from my memory,
the present was tranquil, and the future
gilded by bright rays of hope
and anticipations of joy.

MARY WOLLSTONECRAFT SHELLEY

Perseverance

*Continue in the faith firmly established
and steadfast, and not moved away from the
hope of the gospel that you have heard, which
was proclaimed in all creation under heaven.*

COLOSSIANS 1:23 NASB

During a recent storm with high winds,
several trees were uprooted, damaging homes,
outbuildings, and vehicles and taking down
power lines and knocking out electricity in the
process of their fall. On the surface, the trees
looked strong. But when the strong winds came,
their roots were too shallow to hold the trees up.

Twice in scripture we're given a picture of a steadfast person who has firmly grounded herself in the Word. She is compared to a tree planted by water that has its roots extended deep into the ground, not depending on the surface water alone. It is not easily uprooted during the storms and winds of life. Instead it thrives in times of drought, putting out new leaves each spring and bearing abundant fruit each season.

The person who embraces the hope of the Gospel spends time in the Word and in prayer, stands firm in the storms, and will not give in to the winds that threaten to uproot it. Instead she digs her roots further into the ground and concentrates on producing fruit. Paul encouraged the Colossians to be mighty-tree believers in spite of the winds of persecution that threatened the very life of the early church. We, too, should be strong, gaining strength in the Gospel, nurturing our souls, and nourishing others.

But as for me, I will hope continually,
and will praise You yet more and more.
PSALM 71:14 NASB

When everything was hopeless, Abraham
believed anyway, deciding to live not on
the basis of what he saw he couldn't do but
on what God said he would do.
ROMANS 4:18 MSG

But Christ, as the Son, is in charge of God's entire
house. And we are God's house, if we keep our
courage and remain confident in our hope in Christ.
HEBREWS 3:6 NLT

Mighty Trees

Father, when the storms of life blow into our lives, we want to stand strong. But that doesn't happen quickly. We bend, and it seems we will break under the pressure life brings. Yet You have promised that those who spend time in Your Word and in prayer will be steadfast in the midst of trials. Make us like trees planted by the water, digging deep for nourishment, resting in Your strength. Amen.

We can rejoice, too, when we run into problems and trials, for we know that they help us develop endurance. And endurance develops strength of character, and character strengthens our confident hope of salvation. And this hope will not lead to disappointment. For we know how dearly God loves us, because he has given us the Holy Spirit to fill our hearts with his love.

ROMANS 5:3–5 NLT

For his anger lasts only a moment, but his favor lasts a lifetime; weeping may stay for the night, but rejoicing comes in the morning.

PSALM 30:5 NIV

Learn from yesterday, live for today, hope for tomorrow. The important thing is not to stop questioning.

ALBERT EINSTEIN

Most of the important things in the world have been accomplished by people who have kept on trying when there seemed to be no hope at all.

DALE CARNEGIE

Hope begins in the dark, the stubborn hope that if you just show up and try to do the right thing, the dawn will come. You wait and watch and work; you don't give up.

ANNE LAMOTT

Nothing More Than Feelings

· ·

LORD, sustain me as you promised, that I may live!
Do not let my hope be crushed.
PSALM 119:116 NLT

Whatever our foe—unemployment, rejection, loss, illness—we may feel beaten down by life. Hope feels crushed by the relentless boulder bearing down on our souls. We think that we can't possibly endure another day. Yes, we feel, we feel. But feelings are often deceiving. God promises to sustain us, to strengthen us, so that we might withstand that massive rock. We can trust Him. He will not allow us to be crushed!

Fixed Hope

Lord, it seems so many believers waver in the face of criticism, intolerance, and persecution. How easy it is for us to take our eyes off the hope that is coming the hope of the revelation of Jesus Christ at His Second Coming, the hope of eternal life with You in heaven. The cares of life crowd out the time we used to spend with You. Restore hope. Prepare us for action. Amen.

Therefore, prepare your
minds for action,
keep sober in spirit,
fix your hope completely
on the grace to be brought to you
at the revelation of Jesus Christ.
1 PETER 1:13 NASB

And our hope for you is firmly
grounded, knowing that as you are
sharers of our sufferings, so also you
are sharers of our comfort.
2 CORINTHIANS 1:7 NASB

We remember before our God and
Father your work produced by faith,
your labor prompted by love,
and your endurance inspired
by hope in our Lord Jesus Christ.
1 THESSALONIANS 1:3 NIV

When I stand before God at the end of my life, I would hope that I would not have a single bit of talent left, and could say, "I used everything you gave me."

ERMA BOMBECK

In a mood of faith and hope my work goes on. A ream of fresh paper lies on my desk waiting for the next book. I am a writer and I take up my pen to write.

PEARL S. BUCK

Hope is the struggle of the soul, breaking loose from what is perishable, and attesting her eternity.

HERMAN MELVILLE

Three things will last forever—
faith, hope, and love.
1 Corinthians 13:13 nlt

Pay close attention to yourself and
to your teaching; persevere in these things,
for as you do this you will ensure salvation
both for yourself and for those who hear you.
1 Timothy 4:16 nasb

Pursue righteousness, godliness, faith,
love, perseverance and gentleness.
1 Timothy 6:11 nasb

Reliance

> *"But blessed are those who trust in the LORD*
> *and have made the LORD their hope and confidence."*
> JEREMIAH 17:7 NLT

"I want you to go to my mountain and offer
your son Isaac as a burnt offering to me."

When God spoke these words to Abraham,
we're not told of his initial reaction to those
words, or if there was one. In Genesis 22,
the words immediately following God's
command are "So, Abraham [obeyed]." He
followed God's instructions to the letter. Even
when Isaac questioned his father about the lack
of a sacrifice, Abraham's only answer was "God
will provide Himself an offering." And God did.
But not until Abraham had tied up his son, laid
him on the altar, and had the knife held high
ready to plunge it into the son of promise.

What amazing faith! But it didn't happen overnight. Abraham's faith grew strong over many years of hearing God command and obeying without hesitation. The writer of Hebrews tells us, "Abraham figured that if God wanted to, he could raise the dead. In a sense, that's what happened when he received Isaac back, alive from off the altar" (11:19 MSG). God had already given them Isaac when Sarah's body was long past the age of childbearing. Abraham believed God when He first told Him he would be the father of many nations, and God counted it as righteousness. And God fulfilled His promise to Abraham, blessing him many times over for his implicit reliance on God.

*But the eyes of the LORD are on those
who fear him, on those whose hope
is in his unfailing love.*
PSALM 33:18 NIV

*Yet you brought me out of the womb;
you made me trust in you,
even at my mother's breast.*
PSALM 22:9 NIV

*Through Christ you have come to trust
in God. And you have placed your
faith and hope in God because
he raised Christ from the dead
and gave him great glory.*
1 PETER 1:21 NLT

*For thou art my hope, O Lord GOD:
thou art my trust from my youth.*
PSALM 71:5 KJV

A man with a grain of faith in God
never loses hope, because he
ever believes in the ultimate
triumph of Truth.

MAHATMA GANDHI

To hope means to be ready at
every moment for that which is
not yet born, and yet not become
desperate if there is no birth
in our lifetime.

EMILY DICKINSON

I'm possessed of a hope
that is steadfast and sure,
Since Jesus came into my heart!
And no dark clouds of doubt
now my pathway obscure,
Since Jesus came into my heart!

RUFUS H. MCDANIEL

Climb In

• • • • • • • • • •

May the God of hope fill you with all joy and peace
as you trust in him, so that you may overflow
with hope by the power of the Holy Spirit.

ROMANS 15:13 NIV

Trust is the bottom line when it comes to living
an abundant life. We will never escape the
muddy ruts without trusting that God
has the leverage and power to pull us out of
the quagmire. They say faith is like believing
the tightrope walker can cross the gorge
pushing a wheelbarrow. Trust is climbing into
his wheelbarrow. Only when we climb into
God's wheelbarrow can His joy and peace
overflow as hope into our hearts.

Implicit Faith

Father, You are wholly trustworthy. Reading through the Hall of Faith in Hebrews 11 reinforces that truth. There is no reason to doubt Your goodness or purposes when You ask us to do something that makes no sense to our human minds. You promise great blessing for those who trust You wholly, one of which is filling us with hope in Christ Jesus. You are greatly to be praised. Amen.

O my God, I trust, lean on, rely on,
and am confident in You. Let me not
be put to shame or [my hope in You]
be disappointed; let not my enemies
triumph over me.
PSALM 25:2 AMP

We put our hope in the LORD.
He is our help and our shield.
In him our hearts rejoice, for
we trust in his holy name. Let your
unfailing love surround us, LORD,
for our hope is in you alone.
PSALM 33:20–22 NLT

O God. . .You. . .are the confidence
and hope of all the ends of the earth
and of those far off on the seas.
PSALM 65:5 AMP

116

*Those who trust in, lean on, and
confidently hope in the Lord are like
Mount Zion, which cannot be moved
but abides and stands fast forever.*
PSALM 125:1 AMP

*For the law never made anything
perfect. But now we have confidence
in a better hope, through which
we draw near to God.*
HEBREWS 7:19 NLT

*So trust in the Lord
(commit yourself to Him,
lean on Him, hope confidently
in Him) forever; for the Lord God
is an everlasting Rock
[the Rock of Ages].*
ISAIAH 26:4 AMP

True Success

"For I know the plans I have for you," declares the
LORD, *"plans to prosper you and not to harm you,*
plans to give you hope and a future."
JEREMIAH 29:11 NIV

As little girls, we dream about the handsome
man we'll one day marry, exciting trips we'll
take, the mansion we'll call home, and the
beautiful, perfect children we'll have.
A successful life—isn't that what we hope for?
But God doesn't call us to be successful;
He calls us to trust Him. We may never be
successful in the world's eyes, but trust in
our Father's omnipotence ensures our future
and our hope. And that's true success.

No Matter What

Lord God, we desire the faith of those women of God who have gone before us. Sarah, the mother of Isaac; Deborah, the judge; Hannah who prayed for a son and then dedicated him to You; Mary, the mother of Jesus; Esther, the Persian queen who saved her nation from Haman's schemes; and so many more. No matter what, faith in You is much more satisfying than relying on ourselves.
We love You.

[I do it because, though He slay me,
yet will I wait for and trust Him and]
behold, He will slay me;
I have no hope—nevertheless, I will
maintain and argue my ways before
Him and even to His face.

JOB 13:15 AMP

I pray that God, the source of hope,
will fill you completely with joy and
peace because you trust in him. Then
you will overflow with confident hope
through the power of the Holy Spirit.

ROMANS 15:13 NLT

And again He says, My trust and
assured reliance and confident hope
shall be fixed in Him.

HEBREWS 2:13 AMP

I believe the single most significant decision I can make on a day-to-day basis is my choice of attitude. It is more important than my past, my education, my bankroll, my successes or failures, fame or pain, what other people think of me or say about me, my circumstances, or my position. Attitude keeps me going or cripples my progress. It alone fuels my fire or assaults my hope. When my attitudes are right, there is no barrier too high, no valley too deep, no dream too extreme, no challenge too great for me.

CHARLES R. SWINDOLL

*God can't break his word. And because his
word cannot change, the promise is likewise
unchangeable. We who have run for our very
lives to God have every reason to grab the
promised hope with both hands and never
let go. It's an unbreakable spiritual lifeline,
reaching past all appearances right
to the very presence of God.*

HEBREWS 6:18–19 MSG

*For we. . .by faith anticipate and wait
for the blessing and good for which our
righteousness and right standing with God
[our conformity to His will in purpose,
thought, and action, causes us] to hope.*

GALATIANS 5:5 AMP

Renewal

*So each generation should set its hope anew on God,
not forgetting his glorious miracles
and obeying his commands.*
PSALM 78:7 NLT

Raising children to be godly has never been
easy, but today's world is changing so quickly
parents have the difficult job of keeping up.
Most young adults, let alone the children,
have no concept of what it was like to grow
up without the technology that gives us
instant access to any kind of information
or entertainment we could want. Setting up
limits and enforcing them is more challenging
every day.

But scripture says each generation is to make its own decision about God. In order to do so, children need to hear about God's miracles, His faithfulness in every situation. They need to learn the importance of obeying God's commands. And the only way they will is if their parents and other adults give testimony of what God has done and is doing in their lives. Our young people need to be exposed to the truths of scripture and the stories of God's working through the ages—from Creation through the events revealed in the book of Revelation. Most of all, this generation needs to see obedience to God's Word.

As the older generation, we must be in the Word ourselves to know what God requires of us, to be renewed daily, so we can correctly portray God before the younger generation. The responsibility rests on us.

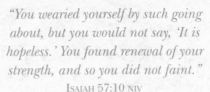

"You wearied yourself by such going about, but you would not say, 'It is hopeless.' You found renewal of your strength, and so you did not faint."

ISAIAH 57:10 NIV

There I will give her back her vineyards, and will make the Valley of Achor a door of hope.

HOSEA 2:15 NIV

*

Return to the stronghold,
O prisoners who have the hope; this very day I am declaring that I will restore double to you.

ZECHARIAH 9:12 NASB

And everyone who has this hope fixed on Him purifies himself, just as He is pure.

1 JOHN 3:3 NASB

What oxygen is to the lungs,
such is hope to the meaning of life.

EMIL BRUNNER

By reading the scriptures I am
so renewed that all natures seem
renewed around me and with
me. The sky seems to be a pure,
a cooler blue, the trees a deeper
green. The whole world is charged
with the glory of God and I feel fire
and music under my feet.

THOMAS MERTON

Expect to have hope rekindled.
Expect your prayers to be
answered in wondrous ways.
The dry seasons of life do not last.
The spring rains will come again.

SARAH BAN BREATHNACH

Cool Summer Shower

. . . .

He will renew your life and
sustain you in your old age.
RUTH 4:15 NIV

Ruth's blessing of renewal is applicable
to us today. *Renovatio* is Latin for "rebirth."
It means casting off the old and embracing the
new: a revival of spirit, a renovation of attitude.
Something essential for women to espouse
every day of their lives. Like a cool rain shower
on a sizzling summer day, Ruth's hope was
renewed by her Lord's touch, and ours will be,
too, if we look to Him for daily replenishing.

Renewed Minds

Father, scripture tells us we must
be renewed by the transformation
of our minds. Our natural sin
nature keeps us from desiring
this until we accept Your gift of
salvation. Knowing Christ and
being in Your Word transforms
our thinking, our actions, and our
feelings. We are new creations,
seeking to draw others to You.
May our goal be as Paul's:
to know You and the power of
Your resurrection. Renew our
minds today. Amen.

*Against its will, all creation
was subjected to God's curse. But
with eager hope, the creation looks
forward to the day when it will join
God's children in glorious freedom
from death and decay.*

ROMANS 8:20–21 NLT

❋

*But those who wait for the Lord
[who expect, look for, and hope in
Him] shall change and renew their
strength and power; they shall lift their
wings and mount up [close to God]
as eagles [mount up to the sun];
they shall run and not be weary,
they shall walk and not faint
or become tired.*

ISAIAH 40:31 AMP

The phoenix hope, can wing her
way through the desert skies, and
still defying fortune's spite;
revive from ashes and rise.

MIGUEL DE CERVANTES SAAVEDRA

The day the Lord created
hope was probably the same
day he created Spring.

BERN WILLIAMS

Whenever I am tempted,
whenever clouds arise,
When songs give place to sighing,
when hope within me dies,
I draw the closer to Him,
from care He sets me free;
His eye is on the sparrow,
and I know He watches me;
His eye is on the sparrow,
and I know He watches me.

CIVILLA D. MARTIN

Divine Refreshment

*You were tired out by the length of your road,
yet you did not say, "It is hopeless."
You found renewed strength,
therefore you did not faint.*
ISAIAH 57:10 NASB

By the end of each day, most women are
ready to collapse. Tight schedules, relentless
deadlines, and plaguing debts make our daily
roads not just physically tiring but spiritually
draining. Our reserves border on empty.
How encouraging to know that renewed
strength is available through the fountain
that never runs dry. If we fill our buckets with
living water—Bible reading, Christian music,
inspirational books and DVDs—we will not
faint, but enjoy divine refreshment.

Renewed Hope

Father, some days are just plain hard. On those days, it's difficult to get our minds to focus on the truths of Your Word. We fail You. We are tempted to give up, saying, "Life's too hard." On those days, remind us of Your love. Remind us of Your faithfulness in the past. Remind us of the hope we have in Christ that this present world is not our eternal reality.
In Christ's name, amen.

Create in me a pure heart, O God,
and renew a steadfast spirit within me.
PSALM 51:10 NIV

Do not be conformed to this world (this age),
[fashioned after and adapted to its external,
superficial customs], but be transformed
(changed) by the [entire] renewal of your mind
[by its new ideals and its new attitude], so
that you may prove [for yourselves] what is the
good and acceptable and perfect will of God,
even the thing which is good and acceptable
and perfect [in His sight for you].
ROMANS 12:2 AMP

Resurrection

It's because of this sacrificed Messiah, whom
God then raised from the dead and glorified,
that you trust God, that you know
you have a future in God.
1 PETER 1:21 MSG

Christmas and Easter are two of the best-loved
events on the church calendar. Have you ever
pondered on the events surrounding Jesus'
birth like Mary did? So much happened within
a year's time: the angel's announcement,
her cousin Elizabeth's late-in-life pregnancy,
Joseph's near divorce until the angel revealed
the truth of Mary's pregnancy, the journey to
Bethlehem, her son's birth in a lowly stable,
the angel's announcement to the shepherds,
and later the wise men's visit and gifts.

Mary knew her son was the promised Messiah, but was she prepared to see Him cruelly nailed to the cross? Did she remember Anna's praise and Simeon's prophecy when she and Joseph took Jesus to the temple to present Him to the Lord?

Then she followed His public ministry that ended after three short years with an arrest, a mock trial, and crucifixion. What were her thoughts during the three days He was in the tomb? What joy and hope rose in her heart when the women returned with the news that Jesus was alive, resurrected from the dead!

Hallelujah! He is risen! He conquered death so that we might have life. Because of His resurrection we have a sure hope of a future with God.

*"My brothers, I am a Pharisee,
descended from Pharisees. I stand
on trial because of the hope of the
resurrection of the dead."*
ACTS 23:6 NIV

*Christ died for our sins, just as the
Scriptures said. He was buried, and he
was raised from the dead on the third
day, just as the Scriptures said.*
1 CORINTHIANS 15:3–4 NLT

*Then we, the living ones who remain
[on the earth], shall simultaneously be
caught up along with [the resurrected
dead] in the clouds to meet the
Lord in the air; and so always
(through the eternity of the eternities)
we shall be with the Lord!*
1 THESSALONIANS 4:17 AMP

Christ the Lord is risen today, Alleluia!
Sons of men and angels say: Alleluia!
Raise your joys and triumphs high, Alleluia!
Sing, ye heavens and earth reply: Alleluia!

Lives again our glorious King, Alleluia!
Where, O death, is now thy sting? Alleluia!
Dying once He all doth save, Alleluia!
Where thy victory, O grave? Alleluia!

Soar we now where Christ has led, Alleluia!
Following our exalted Head, Alleluia!
Made like Him, like Him we rise, Alleluia!
Ours the cross, the grave, the skies, Alleluia!

CHARLES WESLEY

Hope Resurrected

*We had hoped that he would be the one
to set Israel free! But it has already been
three days since all this happened.*
LUKE 24:21 CEV

The scenario for this scripture is quite
unusual. Two of Jesus' disciples are describing
their lost hope due to the events surrounding
Jesus' death to none other than Jesus Himself.
They don't recognize Him as they walk
together on the road to Emmaus after
His resurrection. Spiritual cataracts
blind them to the hope they thought
was dead—right in front of them!
Let's open our spiritual eyes to Jesus,
who is walking beside us.

Rejoice!

Father, wow! Just thinking of Christ's perfect sacrifice on the cross and His resurrection lifts our spirits with joy and hope in the future. Without the resurrection we would have no hope, and as Paul said, we would be the most miserable of people. But we are not in despair. We serve a risen Savior. He's alive and with us today and every day. We rejoice in a hope that is eternal. Praise God!

*"And I admit to living in hopeful
anticipation that God will raise the
dead, both the good and the bad.
If that's my crime, my accusers
are just as guilty as I am."*
ACTS 24:15 MSG

*Jesus said to her, I am
[Myself] the Resurrection
and the Life. Whoever believes in
(adheres to, trusts in, and relies on)
Me, although he may die,
yet he shall live.*
JOHN 11:25 AMP

*Therefore my heart rejoiced and
my tongue exulted exceedingly;
moreover, my flesh also will dwell
in hope [will encamp, pitch its tent,
and dwell in hope in anticipation
of the resurrection].*
ACTS 2:26 AMP

Those who hope for no other
life are dead even for this.

JOHANN WOLFGANG VON GOETHE

I have suffered too much in this
world not to hope for another.

JEAN-JACQUES ROUSSEAU

We have always held to the hope,
the belief, the conviction that
there is a better life, a better
world, beyond the horizon.

FRANKLIN D. ROOSEVELT

Earth to earth, ashes to ashes,
dust to dust; in sure and
certain hope of the Resurrection
into eternal life.

BOOK OF COMMON PRAYER

That Morning

· · · · · · · · · · · · · · · ·

You have placed your faith
and hope in God because he raised Christ
from the dead and gave him great glory.
1 PETER 1:21 NLT

Have you ever wondered how Mary felt
that Easter morning when she discovered
Jesus' tomb empty? Already grieving, imagine
the shock of discovering the body of her
Savior—the One who held all her hopes and
dreams—gone! How can that be? Maybe. . . ?
Hope glimmers. But no—impossible.
He did say something about resurrection,
but that was figurative, wasn't it? Who are. . .
You are? I must run and tell them. It's true!
He has risen! He's alive! My hope lives, too!

Our Redeemer Lives

Father God, we stand amazed in Your presence, wondering at the pure, unconditional, and vast love that caused You to send Your only Son to die for our sins. But You didn't leave Him in the grave. You raised Him up into new life, so that we might be raised with Him, alive in the hope of the Gospel. May our lives be a continual symphony of praise because He is our risen Lord. Amen.

"Now I am on trial because of my hope in
the fulfillment of God's promise made to our
ancestors. In fact, that is why the twelve tribes of
Israel zealously worship God night and day, and
they share the same hope I have. Yet, Your Majesty,
they accuse me for having this hope!"
ACTS 26:6–7 NLT

Christ died and rose again for this very purpose—
to be Lord both of the living and of the dead.
ROMANS 14:9 NLT

For I know that my redeemer liveth.
JOB 19:25 KJV

Salvation

Put your hope in the Lord, for with the Lord is
unfailing love and with him is full redemption.
PSALM 130:7 NIV

Redemption is an amazing word—but one
that in English doesn't begin to define all that
is wrapped up in the Greek. In the ancient
Roman and Greek societies, slavery was
common. As the spoils of war, many slaves
came to their masters as children. They knew
no other way of life. The fortunate ones were
bought by good masters, ones who treated
them fairly yet expected good return for the
purchase price. The not-so-fortunate found
themselves in the slave market over and over.
They knew the humiliation of being judged
according to their size, their skills, or their
beauty. Very few slaves had the guarantee they
were bought never to be sold again.

That's one of the meanings of redemption—one that Paul stressed in his writing. Full redemption means the new owner paid the full price for a slave and then set the slave free, never to be sold again. That's what Jesus did when He paid our redemption price on the cross. He paid the ransom price our sin demanded, and redeemed us from the slave market of sin. . .never to be sold again. Whenever the accuser points out our sin, Christ stands before the Judge to show His wounded hands—proof that He paid the slave price—and claims us as His own. Hope placed in Jesus Christ is never disappointed. He has guaranteed our freedom forever.

Therefore, having been justified by
faith, we have peace with God through
our Lord Jesus Christ, through whom
also we have obtained our introduction
by faith into this grace
in which we stand; and we exult
in hope of the glory of God.
ROMANS 5:1–2 NASB

Our worship of idols on the hills
and our religious orgies on the
mountains are a delusion.
Only [hope] in the LORD our God
will Israel ever find salvation.
JEREMIAH 3:23 NLT

For we through the Spirit, by faith,
are waiting for the hope
of righteousness.
GALATIANS 5:5 NASB

My hope is in the Lord
Who gave Himself for me,
And paid the price of
all my sin at Calvary.
For me He died,
For me He lives,
And everlasting life
and light He freely gives.

NORMAN J. CLAYTON

Our hope is in no
other save in Thee;
Our faith is built upon
Thy promise free;
Lord, give us peace,
and make us calm and sure,
That in Thy strength
we evermore endure.
"I Greet Thee, Who My Sure
Redeemer Art"

JOHN CALVIN

Patience of Hope

* * * * * * * * * * * * * * * *

We call to mind your work of faith, your labor of love, and your patience of hope in following our Master, Jesus Christ, before God our Father.
1 Thessalonians 1:3 msg

Labor. The word alone draws a shudder from the most stalwart of pregnant women. Just as laboring to bring forth new physical life requires patience, birthing new spiritual life may require an intensive labor of love: ceaseless prayer. Countless mothers on their knees praying for the salvation of a loved one have rejoiced in answered prayer. Their secret? Patience of hope.

Amazing Love

Father God, what amazing
love You demonstrated toward
us! Because of Your holiness
You cannot tolerate sin in Your
presence. Long before You created
the world, You had a relationship
with us in mind. You knew
Adam and Eve would fall, so You
provided the solution. You would
send Your Son into the world to
pay the awful price demanded by
sin. Because of Jesus' sacrifice
and resurrection, we are now
Your children, righteous
and holy before You.

I am worn out waiting for your rescue,
but I have put my hope in your word.
PSALM 119:81 NLT

The LORD is good unto them that wait
for him, to the soul that seeketh him.
It is good that a man should both
hope and quietly wait for the
salvation of the LORD.
LAMENTATIONS 3:25–26 KJV

But as for me, I will look to the
Lord and confident in Him I will
keep watch; I will wait with hope
and expectancy for the God of my
salvation; my God will hear me.
MICAH 7:7 AMP

This is all my hope and peace,
Nothing but the blood of Jesus.

ROBERT LOWRY

I'm possessed of a hope that
is steadfast and sure,
Since Jesus came into my heart!
And no dark clouds of doubt
now my pathway obscure,
Since Jesus came into my heart!

RUFUS H. MCDANIEL

Do a Little Dance

• • • • • • • • • • • • • • • • • •

*Then Miriam the prophet, Aaron's sister,
took a tambourine and led all the women as
they played their tambourines and danced.*
EXODUS 15:20 NLT

Can you imagine the enormous celebration
that broke out among the children of
Israel when God miraculously saved them
from Pharaoh's army at the Red Sea? Even
dignified prophetess Miriam grabbed her
tambourine and cut loose with her girlfriends.
Despite adverse circumstances, she heard
God's music and did His dance. Isn't that our
goal today? To hear God's music above the
world's cacophony and do His dance as we
recognize everyday miracles in our lives?

Living Godly Lives

Precious Lord, we thank You for the presence of the Holy Spirit who teaches us how to live godly in this ungodly world. When we accept Your free gift of salvation, made possible through the sacrifice of Your Son, You give us everything we need to live godly lives. When we are weak, You give us power to overcome even the strongest of temptations. Words alone will never express our gratitude for such a gift. Amen.

My rightness and justice are near,
My salvation is going forth,
and My arms shall rule the peoples;
the islands shall wait for and expect Me,
and on My arm shall they trust
and wait with hope.

Remember your leaders. . .who brought to you
the Word of God. . . . Imitate their faith (their
conviction that God exists and is. . .the Provider
and Bestower of eternal salvation through Christ,
and their leaning of the entire human personality on
God in absolute trust and confidence in His power,
wisdom, and goodness).

Shelter

In You, O Lord, do I put my trust and seek refuge;
let me never be put to shame or
[have my hope in You] disappointed;
deliver me in Your righteousness!
PSALM 31:1 AMP

David's popularity with the people of Israel
soon turned King Saul's favor away from
him. Saul didn't know that David had been
anointed king in his place. It may not have
made any difference if he had known. But
it mattered to David that Saul was anointed
before him, and therefore he honored Saul
and refused to kill the Lord's anointed, even
when David feared for his life.

Many of David's psalms were written from his hiding places in the wilderness. When Saul's fury led him to attempt murdering David to rid himself of the nuisance, still David refused to retaliate.

Several times David's men urged him to kill Saul when offered the chance. But David was willing to wait on God's timing.

However, there were times when David wondered how much longer the chase could go on. He was tired of keeping one step ahead of Saul. David quickly learned that God was his only true refuge.

Today we still have the hope that God will shelter us from the storms of life. He is always faithful in providing a way of escape when the burdens get too heavy to bear. With God as our refuge we need never to lose our hope that the future belongs to Him. He will shelter us forever from our enemies.

Having hope will give you courage.
You will be protected
and will rest in safety.
JOB 11:18 NLT

LORD, don't terrorize me!
You alone are my hope in
the day of disaster.
JEREMIAH 17:17 NLT

Those who live in the shelter of the
Most High will find rest in the shadow
of the Almighty. This I declare about
the LORD: He alone is my refuge,
my place of safety; he is my God,
and I trust him.
PSALM 91:1–2 NLT

So trust him absolutely, people;
lay your lives on the line for him.
God is a safe place to be.
PSALM 62:8 MSG

Our God, our help in ages past,
Our hope for years to come,
Our shelter from the stormy blast,
And our eternal home.

Our God, our help in ages past,
Our hope for years to come,
Be Thou our guard
while troubles last,
And our eternal home.

ISAAC WATTS

In all things it is better to hope
than to despair.

JOHANN WOLFGANG VON GOETHE

My Refuge

God is our refuge and strength,
always ready to help in times of trouble.
PSALM 46:1 NLT

What is your quiet place? The place you go
to get away from the fray, to chill out, think,
regroup, and gain perspective? Mine is a
hammock nestled beneath a canopy of oaks
in my backyard. . .nobody around but birds,
squirrels, an occasional wasp, God, and me.
There I can pour out my heart to my Lord,
hear His comforting voice, and feel His
strength refresh me. We all need a quiet place.
God, our refuge, will meet us there.

Perfect Refuge

Lord God, You are our shelter, a solid rock, our fortress, our shield, and our strength. You shelter us under Your wings away from the heat of the day and the storm and rain. Your very presence shelters us safe from the enemy's reach. When You tuck us away in Your refuge, You promise us perfect peace because our minds are fixed on You. Quiet and secure. We praise You, Father.

The LORD is my solid rock, my fortress,
my rescuer. My God is my rock—I take
refuge in him!—he's my shield and
my salvation's strength, my place of
safety and my shelter. My savior!
Save me from violence!
2 SAMUEL 22:2–3 CEB

It will be a shelter and shade from
the heat of the day, and a refuge and
hiding place from the storm and rain.
ISAIAH 4:6 NIV

"They are before the throne of God and
serve him day and night in his temple;
and he who sits on the throne will
shelter them with his presence."
REVELATION 7:15 NIV

The Lord's our Rock,
in Him we hide,
A Shelter in the time of storm;
Secure whatever ill betide,
A Shelter in the time of storm.

VERNON J. CHARLESWORTH

Be Thou my battle Shield,
Sword for the fight;
Be Thou my Dignity,
Thou my Delight;
Thou my soul's Shelter,
Thou my high Tower:
Raise Thou me heavenward,
O Power of my power.

DALLAN FORGAILL

Slathered in SPF

· · · · · · · · · · · · · · · · · · · ·

You are my refuge and my shield;
I have put my hope in your word.
PSALM 119:114 NIV

These days, the word shield evokes images of
glistening sunbathers dotting beaches and
carefree children slathered in sunscreen.
Like the psalmist's metal shield, sunscreen
deflects dangerous rays, preventing them from
penetrating vulnerable skin—higher SPF for
more protection. When we are immersed in
God's Word, we erect a shield that deflects
Satan's attempts to penetrate our weak flesh.
Internalizing more of God's Word creates a
higher SPF: Scripture Protection Factor.
Are you well coated?

Protection

Father God, the battle is fierce,
and we are weary. You promise to
be our shield, our protection in the
midst of the war. When our arms
grow weak from exertion and we
are unable to hold our own shields,
You raise Your Word as a shield,
deflecting every fiery dart the
enemy showers on us. And when
the battle is over, You take us into
Your tower of refuge so we can
recoup our strength. We love You.

But you are a tower of refuge to the poor, O Lord,
a tower of refuge to the needy in distress. You are a
refuge from the storm and a shelter from the heat.
For the oppressive acts of ruthless people
are like a storm beating against a wall.

Isaiah 25:4 nlt

"As for God, His way is blameless;
the word of the Lord is tested;
He is a shield to all who take refuge in Him."

2 Samuel 22:31 nasb

I have taken my refuge in you, my Lord God,
so I can talk all about your works!

Psalm 73:28 ceb

Spiritual Growth

I pray that your hearts will be flooded with
light so that you can understand the confident
hope he has given to those he called—his holy people
who are his rich and glorious inheritance.
EPHESIANS 1:18 NLT

Looking at family photos and videos of past
events is so much fun. We marvel at how
quickly time has passed and how quickly
things and people have changed. The trees
in the yard were once small but now are tall
and strong. The home we live in has been
remodeled to fit the needs of a growing family.
But when those pictures were taken, time
seemed to stand still. It was hard to imagine a
future time when everything was older.

It's good to take time and reflect on the past because it is only from that perspective that we can measure growth.

Many of us use the first of a new year or a birthday to think back, see where we've been successful, where we've failed or stagnated, and then make goals for growth in the future. Others do it monthly or weekly, though it is hard to see growth in those shorter periods of time.

When we ask, the Lord often puts the strong light of His Word on the particular area of growth we want to examine. In that light there is no shadow; everything is exposed, the good and the bad. And we see more clearly the hope that lights our pathway and keeps us moving forward, confident in our Savior and Lord.

We're not barging in on the rightful work of others, interfering with their ministries, demanding a place in the sun with them. What we're hoping for is that as your lives grow in faith, you'll play a part within our expanding work.
2 Corinthians 10:15 msg

But grow in the grace and knowledge of our Lord and Savior Jesus Christ. To Him be the glory, both now and to the day of eternity. Amen.
2 Peter 3:18 nasb

The righteous shall flourish like the palm tree: he shall grow like a cedar in Lebanon.
Psalm 92:12 kjv

Lord, make me an instrument of your peace; where there is hatred, let me sow love; where there is injury, pardon; where there is doubt, faith; where there is despair, hope; where there is darkness, light; and where there is sadness, joy.

SAINT FRANCIS OF ASSISI

Make no little plans; they have no magic to stir men's blood. . . . Make big plans; aim high in hope and work.

DANIEL H. BURNHAM

Hope unbelieved is always considered nonsense. But hope believed is history in the process of being changed.

JIM WALLIS

Working Out

· · · · · · · · · · · · ·

I will never give up hope or stop praising you.
PSALM 71:14 CEV

Praise is like a muscle; if we don't exercise
it regularly, it becomes weak and atrophied.
But if we flex and extend an attitude of
gratitude daily, praise grows into a strong,
dependable force that nurtures hope and
carries us through the worst of circumstances.
Like Helen Keller, though blind and deaf,
we'll praise our Creator: "I thank God for my
handicaps, for through them, I have found
myself, my work, and my God."

No Standing Still

Father, for a believer there are no
times of stagnation. We're either
moving forward closer to Jesus or
we are slipping away. It is hard
work, but for most of us, we desire
a close, intimate relationship with
Jesus, our Savior. Knowing Him
means we know You. Open our eyes
of understanding to see where we
may be slipping. Enlighten our
minds to turn toward You and
Your Word. Amen.

So come on, let's leave the preschool fingerpainting exercises on Christ and get on with the grand work of art. Grow up in Christ. The basic foundational truths are in place.

HEBREWS 6:1 MSG

Be alert and on your guard; stand firm in your faith (your conviction respecting man's relationship to God and divine things, keeping the trust and holy fervor born of faith and a part of it). Act like men and be courageous; grow in strength!

1 CORINTHIANS 16:13 AMP

We do not want you to become lazy, but to imitate those who through faith and patience inherit what has been promised.

HEBREWS 6:12 NIV

Never stop believing in dreaming,
and never stop dreaming of
believing. That is what gives us
hope, and what keeps us alive.

UNKNOWN

Hope is the companion of power,
and mother of success; for
who so hopes strongly has within
him the gift of miracles.

SAMUEL SMILES

At first people refuse to believe that
a strange new thing can be done,
then they begin to hope it can
be done, then they see it can be
done—then it is done and all the
world wonders why it was
not done centuries ago.

FRANCES BURNETT

New Life

• • • • • • • • • •

God is so good, and by raising Jesus from death,
he has given us new life and a hope that lives on.
1 PETER 1:3 CEV

The words of a song I wrote while pregnant
with my first child exult in the similarities
between new physical life and new spiritual
life in Christ: "New life stirs within me now.
Like a soft breeze, transforming me now. It's a
miracle of love, precious blessing from above.
My heart has taken wings. . .lift me up!"
New life. By the goodness of God, we can
experience this precious transformation no
less miraculous than a baby growing within us.

Renewed Hope

Lord God, as our faith grows so
does our love for You. As our love
increases so does our desire to be
like Christ. Hope is renewed, and
our steps take us forward with
renewed purpose. We begin to see
the plan You have for us, not for
evil but for hope and a future.
Open our spiritual eyes to see Your
blessings each day. We love You.
In Christ's name, amen.

We do not boast therefore, beyond our proper limit, over other men's labors, but we have the hope and confident expectation that as your faith continues to grow, our field among you may be greatly enlarged, still within the limits of our commission.

2 Corinthians 10:15 AMP

Epaphras. . .[is] always striving for you earnestly in his prayers, [pleading] that you may [as persons of ripe character and clear conviction] stand firm and mature [in spiritual growth], convinced and fully assured in everything willed by God.

Colossians 4:12 AMP

Strength

So be strong and courageous,
all you who put your hope in the LORD!
PSALM 31:24 NLT

In the first two chapters of Luke we are
introduced to two boys at their births. One
was born to an older couple who had never
been able to have a child before. An angel
announced his birth to his father who served
in the temple as a priest. When the father
expressed disbelief in what the angel told
him, he was struck dumb until the promised
boy was born and his name was revealed. His
name was John, and he was the forerunner of
the Messiah, the voice who cried out of the
wilderness. In Luke 1:80, we are told "the child
continued to grow and to become strong in
spirit" (NASB).

An angel announced the impending conception of the second boy to a virgin who was betrothed to be married. Soon after, the young mother went to visit her older cousin who was also unexpectedly pregnant. The older woman confirmed the younger was the chosen mother of the promised Messiah. Later, at the urging of the angel, Joseph married Mary and Jesus was born. Luke tells us that this "Child continued to grow and become strong, increasing in wisdom" (2:40 NASB).

God caused both boys to become strong and increase in the skills they would need for their earthly ministries. For all who hope in God, He makes strong, each according to the purpose for which He made us.

Pardon for sin and a
peace that endureth,
Thy own dear presence
to cheer and to guide;
Strength for today and
bright hope for tomorrow,
Blessing all mine,
with ten thousand beside!

THOMAS CHISHOLM

A key to strengthening spiritual muscles
and enduring hardship is finding
strength in the Word of God.

WALTER MARTIN

God's Purpose

Father, You have a purpose for
each of Your children. While You
may not always reveal it to us,
You always work within Your
plan, orchestrating events and
people who will influence us to
follow You with whole hearts. You
equip us and make us strong in the
places where He needs us. Sustain
us with the hope that is ours
because of Jesus. We love You.
Amen.

*Sustain me according to Your word,
that I may live; and do not let
me be ashamed of my hope.*
PSALM 119:116 NASB

*Now may our Lord Jesus Christ
Himself and God our Father,
who has loved us and given us
eternal comfort and good hope by
grace, comfort and strengthen your
hearts in every good work and word.*
2 THESSALONIANS 2:16–17 NASB

*And now I want each
of you to extend that
same intensity toward
a full-bodied hope,
and keep at it till the finish.*
HEBREWS 6:11 MSG